Moses or Christ?

Paul's Reply to Dispensational Error

Charles D. Alexander

J&J Publications

Blacksburg, VA

2019

First published in 1968

PREFACE

He who would understand the prophets had better begin with Paul's Epistle to the Galatians, where he will find that the Church is one in the Old Testament and New, and the New Testament Church is the fulfillment of all prophecy, the very last phase of God's redemptive work on earth.

He will discover in Galatians who the true Israel is, to whom the promises are made and that there is no other Israel, and no further fulfillment of prophecy.

The problem of the Galatian believers was the conspiracy to impose upon them Jewish interpretations of prophecy, and to claim over them a Jewish priority or privilege. Paul repulses this conspiracy with unparalleled severity.

On this question it was *"Paul contra mundum"* (Paul against the world) as later it was to be, on another vital question, *"Athanasius contra mundum."* Even Peter came under his lash- *"I withstood him to the face because he was to be blamed"* (Galatians 2:1 1). Great men were temporarily swept away by the Jewish pretensions to perpetual privilege and priority — *"Even Barnabas was carried away with their dissimulation"* (Galatians 2:13).

Here Paul placed his foot, the last man on earth to stand between Judaistic heresy and the safety of the church: *"To whom we gave place by subjection, no, not for an hour, that the truth of the gospel might continue with you"* (Galatians 2:5).

In our day the same Jewish heresies have well-nigh crushed the theology of the evangelical churches and destroyed effective preaching of the Word. The error has taken different forms in our time, but springs from the same Judaistic root whose fundamental ground is that Jewish privilege and priority are perpetual and that the New Testament Church at best is only a makeshift arrangement of providence to tide over the time until the resources of a baffled and well-nigh impotent Godhead are assembled in sufficient force to compel at last a Jewish solution of the problem of redemption.

A glance at any average missionary magazine dedicated to Jewish evangelization will clearly show this. Sayings of present Jewish leaders are eagerly quoted in justification of 2,000 years of Jewish unbelief, as showing that the Jewish expectation of a Messianic kingdom on earth, with restoration of temple, sacrifices, and priesthood, is a true interpretation of prophecy, whereas it was because John the Baptist and Christ did not proclaim such a kingdom of earthly and visible Jewish glory and privilege that the one was betrayed to Herod and the other was crucified by Pilate.

Let the martyrdom of John and the crucifixion of the Savior stand for ever as the final answer to that interpretation of prophecy which displaces the church, relegates the gospel, and establishes for *"Israel after the flesh"* an earthly empire and a national economy falsely regarded as *"the kingdom of Heaven."*

The fact that some (but by no means all) earlier Reformed theologians and expositors have given some countenance to the error is neither here nor there; for to a man, they all lived before that final dispensational arrangement of prophecy which has turned error into a heresy.

With happy lack of consistency, the earlier theologians held their post-millennial teachings alongside a truly spiritual interpretation of prophecy, not perceiving that the two were mutually exclusive. Their hearers at least got the benefit of both worlds even though one had to be proved false by the other.

Today, we are not permitted that luxury. The theory has become sinister and subversive through its elaboration into a succession of "ages" to which belong certain well-defined segments of Holy Scripture, all combining to exclude "the church" from all but a fragment of the Divine Word. The Jewish theory predominates. A variety of second comings and last judgments has been invented. The abolition of the gospel has been proclaimed with great enthusiasm for it is fundamental to pre-millennialism that another gospel known as "the gospel of the kingdom" will take the place of the gospel of grace when "the church" is safety removed out of the way.

Paul has a word for those who proclaim "another gospel," or who even proclaim there will ever be another – *"Let him be accursed ... though he be an angel from Heaven"*. (Galatians 1:8)

1

ANOTHER GOSPEL

This perversion of Holy Scripture, now so destructively rife, is significantly at the root of all the modern "cults" which have sprung out of evangelicalism in the last 150 years, all proclaiming "another gospel" which is invariably a thinly concealed doctrine of "works" presented in more orthodox circles under the well-sounding title "Gospel of the Kingdom."

This title occurs very blessedly in the New Testament, of course, but nowhere is it separable from the gospel "kingdom" which is neither here nor there, neither in Jerusalem, nor Samaria, nor Rome, but is *within you* (Luke 17:20-21).

The "Gospel of the Kingdom" as described by our premillennialists is suspiciously like that which the sect known as "Jehovah's Witnesses" proclaims. The inconsistency of former (but otherwise sound) theologians who pursued the millennialist fantasy is testified by our dispensationalists today who indignantly strike from the chapter headings of the Authorized Version of the Bible any reference to "the church" found in those headings throughout the Old Testament prophets.

We are on common ground therefore in acknowledging that the millennialism of the older theologians was inconsistent with modern Dispensationalism or even with more moderate post-millennialism. These men cannot be quoted as experts on prophetical interpretation, but we have every ground for asserting that if they had lived after the invention of the dispensational heresy, they would have fled in dismay from their millennial house and cried havoc!

That Mr. Spurgeon did not appear to perceive this, can only be attributed to the fact that he lived too near the onset of the new error and was too engrossed (rightly so) with the challenge of the new Bible criticism, to perceive the other "downgrade" which after his death became a landslide, and in two generations overwhelmed the evangelical testimony and destroyed theology and divinity, leaving evangelicalism powerless and without nerve or sinew to meet the challenge of world-wide atheism and Satanic unloosing.

We have begun by stating that the key to prophetic understanding of the Old Testament promises lies in the epistle to the Galatians, an epistle specially written to defend the church against all Judaizing errors and interpretations.

The Galatian church was the most Gentile of all the churches of the New Testament, as the name suggests. The inhabitants of that province in Asia Minor were a segment of the great Gaelic-Gaulic-Celtic race from which the English-speaking peoples take most of their blood. It is sad to see that the Judaic-dispensational heresy has found only too congenial ground in this race, as it did in their Asiatic brethren in the days of Paul the apostle. It seems that our race is peculiarly prone to casting away its great privileges and placing its mind in pawn to Judaistic doctrines. *"O foolish Galatians! Who hath bewitched you ...."* (Galatians 3:1).

In Paul's day men came from Judea to Galatia teaching that God had set aside neither the Jewish nation nor Jewish privilege, and unless the Gentiles became as Jews they could not be saved. They even insisted that Gentiles become circumcised as Jews. Against this Paul thundered:

"I testify again to every man that is circumcised that he is a debtor to do the whole law, Christ is become of no effect unto you, whosoever of you are justified by the law; ye are fallen from grace" (Galatians 5:3-4).

It is useless for our friends to tell us that this is not their error, for their interpretations require that in their so-called millennial age Gentiles must be circumcised according to the laws of Ezekiel's "temple." Hence our Savior Christ, supposedly reigning in person in Jerusalem, must preside over the subversion of His own gospel, the undoing of His work of redemption on the Cross and the dismantling of that kingdom of grace and truth which was the sole purpose of His coming into the world. In other words, the "Second Coming" according to the dispensational scheme will undo the whole purpose of the First Coming, and the Law will supplant the gospel.

Those who reject the true spiritual interpretation of Ezekiel 44:6-9 must teach that *"the stranger"* (that is, the Gentile) is to be excluded from God's sanctuary unless he is circumcised. This passage occurs in that portion of Ezekiel in which the New Testament temple is described but which our friends take to mean an actual temple restoration in Jerusalem during the so-called millennial reign of Christ on earth. As they insist that Ezekiel's temple is to be literally constructed they cannot escape the conclusion that circumcision is to be reestablished in their millennium, on a far more extensive scale than ever before; Gentiles must be circumcised as well as Jews if they are to have access to divine worship.

And who is now the heretic - we who plead for a spiritual and gospel interpretation of prophecy, or our friends who reestablish circumcision, the temple, the sacrifice, the Levitical priesthood, and abolish the church and the gospel, and put Moses in the place of Christ?

When we say that the epistle to the Galatians was written to destroy this Judaistic error, we do not overstate the truth, as we shall now attempt to prove.

The third and fourth chapters of Galatians are crucial to the interpretation of prophecy. Three things are shown therein:

(1) The Church is one continuing body in the Old Testament and the New Testament.

(2) The New Testament Church is the fulfillment of Old

Testament prophecy concerning Israel.

(3) Therefore, prophecy concerning the promised kingdom is to be understood in spiritual, not in natural terms.

In the first chapter of Galatians, Paul proves his competence to speak with authority showing that the gospel which he preached and from which the Galatians were in danger of being subverted, was received by him as a direct and specific revelation from God, by-passing all human means, so that his apostleship was not derived from the Jerusalem apostolate with which he had only the flimsiest contact. It was three years after his conversion before he visited Jerusalem, and even then he lived with Peter for only fifteen days, seeing no other apostle save James (the relative of the Lord). His apostleship came direct from Heaven and his knowledge of the gospel from the same exalted source.

He was the man who (whether in spirit or body, he could not say) had been caught up to Heaven and in a personal interview with the glorified Redeemer received that inner knowledge of the divine wisdom in the plan of redemption that exceeded what he was permitted to teach or write (2 Corinthians 12).

In Chapter 2 he records his visit to the great council of the church at Jerusalem called to deal with the Judaistic dispute- a dispute satisfactorily settled in favor of Gentile liberty under the gospel: a liberty unhindered by those Jewish observances which continued amongst the early Jewish believers during the appointed 40 years of Jewish probation terminating with the abolition of the temple, the Mosaic code, the priesthood, sacrifices and the synagogue connection in the Roman war of A. D. 70. In this account of the evangelical council at Jerusalem under the superintendence of the apostle James (Acts 15), the position of the church in relation to the Mosaic Law is clinched by an appeal to the verdict of the prophets themselves. Amos is being quoted as representative of *all* the prophets (note the use of the plural)-Acts 15:15. That Quotation governs the right use of all prophecies related thereto, in reference to the kingdom which Christ came to establish at His first coming, and shows that the kingdom is spiritual and not Jewish, of Heaven and not of earth, and that the rebuilding of David's house has been fulfilled in the perpetual reign of Christ, beginning with the resurrection and the ascension into Heaven.

Though Paul does not recapitulate the history of this great council, he records this result affecting the Gentiles. It was established that Gentile salvation outside the law and outside the Jewish camp was valid, scriptural and eternally binding, though (as Paul declares to his Galatian friends) it would not have mattered to him if the council had gone against him. *"God accepteth no man's person"*. (Galatians 2:6)

Later on Peter came to Antioch and because of fear of the opinion of Judaizing emissaries from James at Jerusalem, compromised with the synagogue faction and separated himself from the Gentiles. Poor Peter! The same Peter who denied his Lord still denies him despite the artificial theories of conference men who declare that Peter was a different man after Pentecost than he was before.

What grandeur in Paul's argument! The final answer to the Judaizing heresy is that the Cross of Christ has abolished the earthly and temporal Jewish economy and set up in its place an economy of the Spirit which transcends the national, the carnal and the external.

"I through the law am dead to the law that I might live unto God. I am crucified with Christ; nevertheless I live..." (Galatians 2:19-20)

2

NO BREAK BETWEEN OLD TESTAMENT AND NEW TESTAMENT

There follows the Pauline analysis of the nature and history of the true church, as contained in chapters 3 and 4, The first great conclusion Paul presents to the Galatians is that the only true children of Abraham, the heirs to the Abrahamic covenant, blessing and promise, are true believers, whether Jew or Gentile:

"Know ye therefore that they which be of faith, the same are the children of Abraham. (Galatians 3:7)

There can be **no appeal** from this fundamental statement. In one sentence Paul destroys the entire dispensational, pre-millennial and post-millennial edifice. It is foundational to all three systems that Jewish privilege and a special Jewish future must be maintained on the basis that the Abrahamic covenant was exclusive to the natural (i.e. Jewish) seed of Abraham.

But Paul shows in these two chapters that the *"seed of Abraham"* is Christ, and that they who are Christ's (and no one else) are *"Abraham's seed and heirs according to the promise"*; that this *"seed"* abolishes all distinction of birth or privilege, for *"there is neither Jew nor Greek, there is neither bond nor free, there is neither male nor female: for all are one in Christ Jesus"*. (See Galatians 3:16, 28, 29).

Moreover, the promise of redemption in Christ took precedence over the law - by 430 years - the time lapse between Abraham and Moses. The Law itself, with its apparatus of temple, priest and sacrifice, was only added *"because of transgression"* to bridge the gap till Christ came. Galatians 3:17-19.

How say our literalists therefore that the temple and Levitical priesthood and sacrifice, are to be restored in the "Millennium"? If they were only established as a discipline to hold iniquity in check until gospel times, who will re-establish them save at the cost of recalling the sin and transgression which they were fitted only to restrain? And who now is the heretic?

Paul goes further and shows by the nature and history of the true church that no break has occurred between the Old Testament and New Testament Church. The Church of the New Testament is the legitimate successor of the church of the Old Testament.

Few chapters of Scripture have been so maltreated and

distorted as the third chapter of Galatians. Evangelical expositors have sought to show from the word: *"The Law was our schoolmaster to bring us to Christ,"* that the Holy Spirit uses the Law in evangelical conversion to drive us through conviction of sin into the arms of Christ. Now whatever experimental truth there may be in this, it is not the subject of Paul's argument. The Galatians were never under *"the schoolmaster."* The *"schoolmaster"* is the regime of the Law over Old Testament Israel to preserve the nation in its function as the Church of God in the Old Testament till the *"fullness of times"* when Christ came at His first advent.

"Before faith came we were kept under the law, shut up unto the faith which should afterwards be revealed" (v.23).

This can only mean that the church was under legal restraints and administration till the time of gospel faith, that is, till the time when the fulfillment of the promise in Christ should release the people of God from all earthly and legal restraints and set them free without priest, sacrifice, temple, washings, outward observances or any such *"rudiments of the world,"* to serve God in the spirit.

Christ said to the woman of Samaria: *"Neither in this mountain, nor yet at Jerusalem, shall men worship the Father, but the hour is coming AND NOW IS* [emphasis mine] *when the true worshipers shall worship the Father in spirit and in truth..."* (John 4:21-24)

In these words Christ abolishes temple, priesthood, sacrifice, circumcision and the entire apparatus of the Mosaic Covenant. Though for another 40 years of probation these "rudiments" were permitted to continue (though without legal enforcement) among pious Jews still attached to the nation and the synagogue. The judgment of the Roman war brought all to an end.

Among Gentile believers no such regulations and requirements were to be tolerated. The attempt to impose them was subversive to the gospel itself, the belief so current now among sincere Christians, that the "rudiments" of the Mosaic code will actually, after 2,000 years, be re-imposed not only on the Jew but on the Gentile also, is a heresy which baffles credence.

The thunders of the Galatian epistle notwithstanding, this subversive doctrine has obtained a stranglehold on theological thought and under the form of "Dispensationalism" has vindicated 2,000 years of Jewish unbelief. It must be repelled and repudiated with the utmost vigor if preaching and exposition of the Word of God is to be restored to the church, and in this exercise the Epistle to the Galatians is crucial.

3

THE CHURCH COMES OF AGE

"But after that faith is come, we are no longer under a schoolmaster" (v.25).

The "coming" of faith in the apostle's argument denotes the passage of the church from the Mosaic to the New Testament economy. It is not an individual experience of the sinner coming to the Savior, but a moment in history when the regime of law gave way to the regime of faith, and the *"schoolmaster"* (the apparatus of the law summarized under the term "circumcision") handed over his office to Christ, and the church passed from its "minority" to its "majority."

The conclusion of this chapter (vv. 26-29) is the charter of the New Testament Church and the ground of her invincible claim to be the lawful successor of Abraham, the true Israel, the true circumcision (not in the flesh but in the spirit), the inheritor of the promises and privileges and hope of Old Testament Israel. Hence:

"If ye be Christ's, then are ye Abraham's seed and heirs according to the promise" (v.29).

This glorious sentence winds up the Old Covenant, abolishes the law, the temple, and circumcision, terminates the mission of the Jewish nation, ends their exclusive rights and privileges, and provides the key to the understanding of the Law, the Writings, and the Prophets of the Old Testament.

This one sentence is the death-knell of that dispensational heresy which has filled the Church with the rubbish of a dismantled legalism and aims to re-impose in an age yet to come all those temporalities and restrictions which Christ died once and for all to abolish.

The subtle doctrine that the gospel of Christ's free grace is going to give away to an imagined millennium of re-imposed Jewish privileges, is reinforced by the teaching that there will be in that "golden age" another "gospel" preached, the so-called "gospel of the kingdom" which, whatever way we look at it, becomes a gospel of works and not of grace.

We beg our readers to consider that every false cult or sect which has sprung from the evangelical body in the last century and a half, is dispensational in nature and carries to its logical conclusion this Jewish and rabbinical principle of a gospel of works. It is proclaimed by the "Jehovah's Witnesses" in their significantly named "Kingdom Halls," by

Christadelphians and Adventists, and by the newly developed cult launched by Mr. Herbert Armstrong, a financial wizard who claims to be the only man or organization on earth to be proclaiming the truth, and therefore entitled to all the legalistic "tithes" of the Lord's people. Aptly he has been called, "Mr. Ten Percent."

These outrageous impositions are evangelical in their origin and are only variations of that Dispensationalism which began in the early 19th century, became standardized by Dr. C. I. Scofield in his "reference Bible" and has ever since dominated the evangelical scene.

We cannot proclaim too strongly the dangers of this subtle and incredible movement which now shackles the evangelical mind and destroys all true Bible exposition. It is one of the principal tasks of the movement in our day towards sound Biblical and "Reformed" exposition, to destroy this error. In that task one principal weapon must be the epistle to the Galatians.

4

THE FINAL FORM OF ISRAEL

If we can demonstrate and prove that the Galatian epistle establishes beyond all cavil that the Church is one, a unity, in Old Testament and New Testament, and that therefore the New Testament Church is the final form of "Israel," the inheritor of all the promises to Abraham, Isaac and Jacob, the fulfillment of the prophecies of the kingdom which Messiah came to establish, and did in fact establish, our task will have been completed and our readers must do the rest.

It is our deliberate contention that this is the very position established in the next chapter (the fourth) of our Galatian epistle, established with such force that it can only be avoided by a blindness or an ignorance culpable in its nature.

Chapter four contains Paul's final argument, proving these two things:

(1) That the work of "adoption" performed in the hearts of all true believers demonstrates that they are the legitimate successors of the Israelitish church of the Old Testament.

(2) He reinforces this by an allegory built upon Abraham's history, showing that the natural Jew is not Israel at all but Ishmael; and that the church of Jew and Gentile believers is the true and only and exclusive Israel of God.

This being so, the promises to Israel in the Old Testament prophecies are to be spiritually understood even when they speak apparently of literal and material restoration of "Israel and Judah." This is the key the only key, to prophetical interpretation. We proceed therefore:

Galatian 4: 1 *"Now I say that the heir, as long as he is a child, differeth nothing from a servant though he be lord of all."*

Paul is saying that in Old Testament times the true church, the true people of God, were in a state of minority. Not having "come of age," they were treated as a child in a rich man's household, the heir to all the father's estates and privileges, but not yet at that age when that inheritance could properly be bestowed. Therefore, the child-heir finds himself fenced about with restrictions and officers who regulate his life so that he has no liberty to enjoy his privileges but must await "the time appointed of the Father." This is expressed by Paul in the words, *"But is under tutors and governors until the time appointed of the father"* (Galatians 4:2).

21

The tutors and governors of the church in the Old Testament were the regulations of the Mosaic code. Paul deliberately transfers the figure of the child-heir to the church in her Old Testament minority in the words- *"Even so we, when we were children, were in bond age under the elements* [margin - rudiments] *of the world"* (Galatians 4:3).

The childhood of the church was in Israelitish form under the Old Testament. The "bondage" was the subjection of the people of God to those earthly "rudiments" of visible temple, sacrifices, circumcision, and all other legal observances "in the flesh" which constituted the preparatory condition of the people of God before the coming of Christ. Of that glorious event when the church obtained her release and passed from under the law to the full liberty of gospel faith, Paul now speaks-

"But when the fullness of the time was come, God sent forth His Son, made of a woman, made under the law, to redeem them that were under the law, that we might receive the adoption of sons" (Galatians 4:4-5).

"The fullness of the time" means the times of prophetical fulfillment of all the purposes and promises of God in redemption. That Paul should call the gospel times *"the fullness of the time"* means that the gospel age is the age of fulfillment of all things which God spake by His holy prophets since the world began. (Luke 1:70)

These are *"the last days"* described by Paul in Hebrews 1:2, *"the end of the world"* (Hebrews 9:26), *"the last time"* (1 John 2:18). If these are the last days, and the last time, and the end

Age

of the world, how say the dispensationalists that there is a "time" after "the last time," another kingdom to come after the "kingdom of God" has run its course, another age after the gospel age? We await with confidence their reply.

In this *"fullness of time"* God's Son was sent forth, born of the virgin, born under the law, that as One obliged by His true humanity and the time at which He appeared, to keep the whole law, did so in the perfection of His mediatorial office, redeeming *"those who were under the law"* that they with us Gentiles might receive together that *"adoption of sons"* which sets us beyond the servitude of the law and introduces us to the full inheritance of the sons of God.

"And because ye are sons, God hath sent forth the Spirit of His Son into your hearts crying Abba, Father" (v.6).

This is the difference between the experience of the people of God in the Old Testament and those in the New Testament. The difference is not one of the quality of salvation or the nature of faith, but in the status and privilege enjoyed. Living after the sacrifice of Christ which procured the full restoration of the soul to direct communion with God, the believer now receives the full witness of sonship and is released from the service of outward forms and ceremonies.

5

SARAH AND HAGAR

After remonstrating with the Galatians for yielding so easily to the subversions of Judaistic teachers, Paul resumes his argument in the famous allegory of Sarah and Hagar. This occupies verse 21-31 of our chapter and is the final word to end all argument of prophetical interpretation.

Abraham had two sons - Ishmael and Isaac. The former, who was the son of the bondwoman, Hagar the Egyptian, was rejected by God as not being the true heir. The other, Isaac, was the son of Sarah the true wife, and this was the true seed through whom the promise of God would come.

Then, in the apostle's argument, comes the most startling reversal in the entire history of prophecy.

Hagar, the Egyptian bondmaid, is identified with Jerusalem

and Jewry. Sarah is identified with the true Church *"the heavenly Jerusalem."*

The allegory thus declares that earthly Israel (the twelve tribes) is to be regarded as Ishmael because they are in bondage to the law and not free. The true Church of Gentile and Jew (in which all distinctions of race, degree and privilege are abolished - this is the true Israel to whom the promises made to Abraham apply.

Hagar and Ishmael stand for Jerusalem *"which now is"* (that is, the earthly Jerusalem standing with temple and sacrifice at the time of Paul's writing). Sarah and Isaac stand for the true gospel church, the *"Jerusalem which is from above."* The covenant made with Abraham is the promise of the gospel, and from that promise every Jew alive or who ever will be alive, is excluded except insofar as he comes by the same road of repentance, faith and regeneration which the Gentile believer treads.

Paul reinforces his allegory with a quotation from Isaiah 54:1:

"Rejoice thou barren [Sarah] *that barest not; break forth and cry thou that travailest not: for the desolate* [the New Covenant] *hath many more children than she that hath an husband* [the Old Covenant]."

The abolition of the Old Covenant means the abolition of Israel (Jewry) from all her privileges, and the emergence of the New Testament Church is the rise of the new "Israel of God," Jew and Gentile, with all distinctions obliterated, to whom alone the Abrahamic promises belong.

This is tersely and categorically expressed by the apostle in the words, *"Now we, brethren* [i.e., the church of the N. T.] *as Isaac was, are the children of promise."*

Paul touches in v.29 upon the persecuting envy of the Jews against the church to whom their privileges have passed, and likens it to the hatred of Ishmael against Isaac and concludes his argument by quoting against the Jew the very words originally spoken against Hagar and her son Ishmael:

"Nevertheless what saith the Scripture? Cast out the bondwoman with her son [i.e., the Old Covenant and the earthly Israel]: *for the son of the bondwoman* [Israel] *shall not be heir with the children of the free woman* [that is, the N. T. Church]*"* (v.30).

The dreadful judgment of these words is unmistakable: Israel is cast off and cast off forever as a nation. Paul gives no hint of any "restoration" though here would be the place to state it, if restoration there is to be. Jewish privilege is ended for all time. The covenant has passed to the New Testament Church in which Israel has no part except as individual believers.

This *"casting off"* is not anywhere modified by Paul. We have elsewhere shown that in Romans 11 Paul is speaking of individual Jews and not the nation, when he writes, *"If the casting away of them be the riches of the Gentiles, what shall the receiving of them be but life from the dead?"* His last word to the Galatians is, *"So then brethren, we are not children of the bondwoman, but of the free"* (Galatians 4:3 1).

This he writes to the most Gentile of all the churches,

showing that to the Gentile church has passed the covenant, the glory, the birthright, the privilege and the redemption hope.

The consequences are most far-reaching. They extend to every prophecy of the Old Testament in which the New Covenant is foretold, even though the words of the prophets are addressed to *"Israel and Judah."* That *"Israel and Judah"* is the New Testament Church, and though the prophecies are couched in terms of the land of Israel and employ topographical and geographical details drawn from the earthly territory of the twelve tribes, these are *"figures of the true"* just as temple, sacrifice and priesthood, passover and feasts were *"figures of the true,"* designed to portray gospel truths to those whose ears are open to hear. It is greatly to be feared that to very few of our prophetical teachers today those words could be addressed: *"Blessed are your eyes for they see, and your ears for they hear"* (Matthew 13:16).

It might well be asked of our dispensational friends today, "What was it that the Lord hid from the wise and prudent Jews of His day and revealed only to *"babes"*? (Matthew 11:25) If it were "the things" pertaining to His kingdom which He had come to establish on the ruins of Satan's empire of sin and death, then the "kingdom" which he "offered" to the Jews was entirely spiritual and not natural, and this is the reason why it was concealed from all except those with eyes to see and ears to hear.

The reason why the Jews rejected Christ is the same as that for which they still reject Him today - namely, because they expected an earthly kingdom, and Christ did not bring them this. The prevailing prophetical theories, however, insist that

Christ did in fact "offer" this kingdom to the Jews and because they rejected the offer, the gospel was brought in as an afterthought or a substitute. What the dispensational theory is saying is that Christ offered to the Jews the very kingdom which they expected, but they rejected Him and it! At the last, says this extraordinary theory, Christ will relent and will in fact give the Jews the very kingdom which they crucified Him for not establishing at His first coming. The dispensational theory therefore vindicates the Jew for 2,000 years of unbelief and at the same time contradicts itself by alleging that the kingdom which the Jews rejected was the very kingdom which they crucified Him for not offering but which will be gratuitously conferred upon them in the near future as the fulfillment of what God promised to Abraham.

If our friends cannot see the hopeless dilemma in which their theory involves them, we can only marvel at the success of that error of Dispensationalism by which evil powers have succeeded in well nigh destroying scriptural exposition and understanding.

The truth is that there is not a breath of suggestion that Christ ever "offered" to the Jews any other "kingdom" but the gospel: that this was in fact the kingdom which John the Baptist came to present under the keyword "repent," which Christ Himself presented with the same keyword "repent," that the Sermon on the Mount with which He formally introduced His mission was in fact an exposition of the text, *"Repent, for the kingdom of Heaven is at hand."* In that great sermon Christ promised or offered nothing to anyone except *"the poor in spirit,"* the *"mourner for sin,"* the *"meek,"* the *"brokenhearted,"* and those who *"hungered and thirsted"* for true righteousness.

Dispensationalism, faced with the embarrassment that these dispositions of soul are noticeably absent in the Jewish occupation of Palestine today, had to descend to the device that the Jew must go back to Palestine in unbelief though this was the very reason for which the Jew was cast out of Palestine. The theory teaches that the Second Coming of Christ will convert the Jews *"in a day"* despite the fact that they do not need to be converted to the conceptions of an earthly kingdom of Christ, seeing they crucified the Savior for not setting up this very thing.

The dispensational theory today is jubilantly hailing the prospect of an early fulfillment of Jewish expectation of an earthly kingdom of Messiah. The theorists exceed the rabbis in this enthusiasm, though it is from rabbinical sources that their theory has been contrived. They actually tell the Jews that their present occupation of Palestine, in a state of bitter hostility to Christ and the Christian gospel, is the fulfillment of prophecy and that their ungodly zeal against Christ and truth will be rewarded shortly by God with an instant faith and that this extraordinary act of God will be a fulfilling of the promises made to Abraham.

But Paul in Galatians has already told us who Abraham's seed are, to whom these promises are made, and he mentions not a word about restoration to Palestine, but builds it all on the nature of the Church. He maintains, as we have shown, that the Church is the lawful continuation of Old Testament Israel and the inheritor of the Abrahamic covenant and promises.

We ask our dispensational friends to consider what their

position will be if the present Jewish occupation ends in disaster. While they are forming their reply, we would point out to readers that so far from converting Israel and establishing them in the land, the second coming of Christ will overtake them (and all the world) *"as a thief in the night,"* in the which the heavens will pass away with a great noise and the elements melt with fervent heat, the earth also and the works that are therein shall be burned up (2 Peter 3: 1 0).

Peter knows of no other "second coming" save that which abolishes the heavens and the earth in one stupendous conflagration. Where then is the earthly kingdom which Christ is to bring to the Jew, and where is the "kingdom" of the Jehovah's Witnesses, the Christadelphians, the Adventists and the Armstrongites? We fear for the company which our dispensationalists keep and earnestly entreat them to consider Paul's interpretation of who Israel is, what are *"the two covenants"* and what is the nature of *"the promise"* made to Abraham?

Our last word is that of Paul, significantly found in the conclusion of that epistle specifically written to deliver the Church from Jewish error and Jewish pride:

"God forbid that I should glory, save in the cross of our Lord Jesus Christ, by whom the world is crucified unto me and I unto the world. For in Christ Jesus neither circumcision availeth anything nor uncircumcision, but a new creature. And as many as walk according to this rule, peace be on them, and mercy, AND UPON THE ISRAEL OF GOD." (Galatians 6:14-16)

Made in the USA
Las Vegas, NV
14 July 2023